Tell 21

Prayer. Care. Share.

Timothy Eldred

WITH PAUL WALKER

BroadStreet
PUBLISHING

BroadStreet Publishing Group, LLC
Racine, Wisconsin, USA
BroadStreetPublishing.com

In partnership with EndeavorResources.org

Tell 21: Prayer. Care. Share.

Copyright © 2017 Timothy Eldred

ISBN-13: 978-0-9796-5515-9 (softcover)
ISBN-13: 978-1-4245-5441-6 (e-book)

Stock or custom editions of BroadStreet Publishing titles may be purchased in bulk for educational, business, ministry, fundraising, or sales promotional use. For information, please e-mail info@broadstreetpublishing.com.

Cover by GarborgDesign.com
Interior design and typeset by theDESKonline.com

Printed in the United States of America
17 18 19 20 21 5 4 3 2 1

Contents

Now who is there to harm you if you are zealous for what is good? But even if you should suffer for righteousness' sake, you will be blessed. Have no fear of them, nor be troubled, but in your hearts honor Christ the Lord as holy, always being prepared to make a defense to anyone who asks you for a reason for the hope that is in you; yet do it with gentleness and respect, having a good conscience, so that, when you are slandered, those who revile your good behavior in Christ may be put to shame. For it is better to suffer for doing good, if that should be God's will, than for doing evil. For Christ also suffered once for sins, the righteous for the unrighteous, that he might bring us to God, being put to death in the flesh but made alive in the spirit. (1 Peter 3:13–18)

Introduction

There's a story taking place. It's a tale of epic proportions. An adventure with cosmic connotations. This is a life-altering saga with an intense sense of urgency. And you've been invited to join the cast of this chronicle. Handpicked. Summoned by the Author. God himself has chosen you. Plugged you into the plot.

No, it's not a mistake. Your invitation was planned before you were born. The role was specifically created with you in mind. You're here to be a testimony of God's love that tells his story to the world. That's why God chose you! Not by accident. Completely on purpose.

Before we continue, let's set the record straight. You're a member of the cast. Your performance is important. But this narrative can't be about you. The real star of your story is Jesus Christ. He's the Hero.

God sent Jesus to rescue the earth and to restore the world. He came to deliver all people from a life of slavery, oppression, suffering, and death. Sounding epic yet?

Make no mistake. This isn't a fairy tale. It's a nonfiction fight for freedom. But it's also a love story. Love is the motivating factor in this historic adventure. God is love (1 John 4:8). He doesn't get his way by bullying or making threats of suppression. He doesn't work through manipulation, shame, and fear, like humans. Instead, he gave his Son. And Jesus gave everything in one heroic act on the cross to give you freedom.

By accepting God's love and your role, you also commit to telling others about the world's Rescuer, Jesus, and what he has done in your life. That's your story. And when your story is used for God's benefit, it becomes his story for his purposes.

God doesn't make up the story as he goes along. It's not an improv. There's a plan. A blueprint. And Jesus has been at the center of it from the very beginning (Colossians 1:15–22). His purpose was to give people a way to know God. A way to escape pain, suffering, sin, and death. Even better, a way to have eternal life.

Jesus' teachings defied dictators, rulers, and systems that controlled people. He conquered forces of darkness that fight against the freedom God intended you to have. He came to share a message of love. Of hope. And peace. Sadly, the world rejected him and killed him (John 1:9–13).

But that didn't end the story.

Three days after Jesus sacrificed everything, God brought him back to life (Philippians 2:9–11). His death and resurrection gives us full backstage access to God again. The minute you understand and embrace Jesus' story and its impact on your life is the moment you must prepare to share it with others. That's their ticket to abundant life and eternal freedom.

Now, timing is everything. God is always on schedule (2 Peter 3:9). Your life at this time in history is significant. God arranged for you to happen. He added you to the script. And since you know Jesus, you have an assignment to complete.

So what's your task exactly?

Over the next twenty-one days, you'll learn to tell others how Jesus' story has become the story of your life. You'll have the chance to explain that through God's grace the world has a second chance to know him.

It's this always-available, never-ending gift of grace that compels us to play our part in this plot and accept responsibility to share his story with the world. We shine his light because God made him the center-stage star and main character. It is now, and has always been, all about Jesus!

Is this assignment risky? Of course. But don't worry. Millions of others have been in your shoes. God will give you strength and confidence. He has promised to never let you down (Hebrews 13:15). Remember, you've been purposely picked to help others find Jesus. This little book will help you learn your lines and live out God's purpose for your life.

You've been invited to be a light in this drama. Someday the final curtain will close (Matthew 14:10–14), but right now, you've been enlisted. The clock is ticking, so let's get started.

Time to let your light shine!

Week 1

PRAYER

Prayer

The first week of your twenty-one-day adventure begins by tackling the topic of prayer. During Jesus' life on earth, he spent more than three years training young protégés to tell his story to the world. It required teaching them many important lessons.

One day when he was praying, Jesus' students made a request: "Lord, teach us to pray, just as John taught his disciples" (Luke 11:1 NLT).

They could have asked anything. Like, "How do we heal sick people?" Or, "What's the secret to getting rid of evil spirits?" Even, "Could you please show us the bread-and-fish trick again?" Instead, they desired the most important lesson Jesus could offer, asking, "How do we pray?"

The greatest resources to help you understand God's plan for your life are his Word and prayer. They're direct access through Jesus to *the* Power

Source. By praying, you connect one-on-one with God, who is the Author of the story. He's the one who put everything into motion. He planned for your life and put you on this page. Literally.

God knew you'd be reading *Tell21* today. He's not shocked. He knows you're getting ready to share your Jesus story. And He wants you to talk to him about your assignment. More importantly, he wants you to plug in to him every day as your source of strength. How? By praying. God invites you into a two-way conversation through prayer.

In the Bible, we see Jesus praying for his followers. The night before Jesus was going to be murdered, we find him having dinner with his disciples. At one point, he turns to Peter and says, "Stay on your toes. Satan has tried his best to separate all of you from me, like chaff from wheat. [Peter], I've prayed for you in particular that you not give in or give out. When you have come through the time of testing, turn to your companions and give them a fresh start" (Luke 22:31–32 MSG).

Basically, he says, "I've asked God to give you the strength to tell your story." Really, that's what he means. Jesus knew Peter's friends would go through a rough time. He knew there would be days they felt like giving up. And he knew Peter's story of trusting Jesus to overcome his struggles could change their lives.

You have a story to tell too. And many of your "companions" need "a fresh start" as well. So this Bible verse is for you. Jesus has your back. You really have nothing to fear at all about the part God has asked you to play in his story.

🔦 Spotlight

Have you ever thought, *I'm just one person, so what difference can I make?* If so, you're not alone. Throughout history, countless others have asked the same question. Despite the odds of being alone, they decided to trust God to use them and make an impact.

A few years ago, some Christians visited a country to tell young people about their Hero, Jesus, and the salvation he offers. They walked around neighborhoods. Hosted games. Visited schools. And handed out thousands of books that explained the life and sacrifice of Christ.

One day, the team invited neighborhood children to come to the town's theater for a fun-filled event with all kinds of prizes. This would be a real celebration. On the night of the event, thousands of young people packed the theater. At the pinnacle of the party, one team member stood up and explained that Jesus wanted to play an important role in their lives. So anyone who was ready should stand and come to the front of the stage.

Silence.

No one stood. Or moved. The team prayed for someone to take this important step of courage. Nothing. Nada. No one wanted to walk forward first.

Finally, a young man rose. His friends told him to sit down, but he didn't. So they mocked him.

"I need Jesus!" he shouted. Then he marched to the front with his head high and his heart sure. As he made the walk, hundreds more followed and asked Jesus to take center stage in their lives.

James 5:16 tells us, "Confess your sins to each other and pray for each other so that you may be healed. The earnest prayer of a righteous person has great power and produces wonderful results" (NLT). With prayer and courage, God can work through one. He can work through you. Be contagious. And set the pace for others!

↱ SHARE THIS

You're here to be a testimony of God's love that tells his story to the world. #tell21

Have Patience

The world just keeps moving faster and faster. A push of a button is all it takes to get instant information. How does living in a downloadable world work when it comes to patience and prayer?

📖 Word

[The man in the vision] said, "Don't be afraid, Daniel. Since the first day you began to pray for understanding and to humble yourself before your God, your request has been heard in heaven. I have come in answer to your prayer. But for twenty-one days the spirit prince of the kingdom of Persia blocked my way. Then Michael, one of the archangels, came to help me, and I left him there with the spirit prince of the kingdom of Persia. Now I am here to explain what will happen to your

people in the future, for this vision concerns
a time yet to come." (Daniel 10:12–14 NLT)

👥 Reflect

Daniel didn't have today's technology at his fin-
gertips to give him immediate data on what was
coming his way. When he saw a vision of a troubled future, his only option was to patiently humble
himself before God in prayer. Like you, he had to
wait for God to show up and reveal his plan.

↪ SHARE THIS

God has a plan. Pray for direction to follow
it, patience to wait on it, and knowledge to
know when it comes. #tell21

🔓 Prayer

Lord, I believe you've written me into your story
and given me this important assignment. I know
there will be obstacles during this twenty-one-
day journey. Please help me to be patient as I
commit to pray every day for the right opportunity. Thank you for removing the roadblocks
to telling others about the world's only hope. In
Jesus' name, amen.

Be Persistent

When we pray to an invisible God, it can be hard to believe he's there, he cares, or he's listening. But we must take him at his word. He will answer right on time and in the very best way. Keep praying.

📖 Word

[Jesus] said to them, "Which of you who has a friend will go to him at midnight and say to him, 'Friend, lend me three loaves, for a friend of mine has arrived on a journey, and I have nothing to set before him'; and he will answer from within, 'Do not bother me; the door is now shut, and my children are with me in bed. I cannot get up and give you anything'? I tell you, though he will not get up and give him anything because he is his friend, yet because of his impudence he will rise and give him whatever he needs. And

I tell you, ask, and it will be given to you; seek, and you will find; knock, and it will be opened to you." (Luke 11:5–9)

👥 Reflect

After Jesus taught his students to pray, he told them the story you just read. It was his way of preparing them for those times of doubt and unbelief. The lesson is still true for you today.

Don't get discouraged when God makes you wait. Be faithful, continuing to ask, seek, and knock. Prayer opens doors.

> ### ↪ SHARE THIS
> Faith sees the invisible, believes the un-believable, and receives the impossible.
> #tell21

🔓 Prayer

Lord, I want to believe you're always there. You know my heart, and you hear my prayers. Help me to not become discouraged in the delay. Give me a greater hunger for you. Teach me to be persistent and to trust in your perfect timing so I don't give up when I should keep pushing on. In Jesus' name, amen.

With Purpose

Praying with purpose is asking God to fulfill what he's already begun. Since God's work is always a story, your prayers will be part of his bigger story. Instead of using prayer as a quick fix to get results, your prayer becomes a way of collaborating with God's plan.

📖 Word

[Peter and John said,] "And now, O Lord, hear their threats, and give us, your servants, great boldness in preaching your word. Stretch out your hand with healing power; may miraculous signs and wonders be done through the name of your holy servant Jesus." After this prayer, the meeting place shook, and they were all filled with the Holy Spirit. Then they preached the word of God with boldness. (Acts 4:29–31 NLT)

👥 Reflect

God is the one who wrote you into the script. Your role is to find your place within it and join him in his work. Your prayer today becomes purposeful as you determine whom God is preparing to hear your Jesus story.

🔗 SHARE THIS

The purpose of prayer isn't to get God to bend in your direction but to get you to bend toward him. #tell21

🔒 Prayer

Lord, I'm so blessed to know Jesus as my Hero. Thank you for choosing me and using me for your purpose. My story is your story, and I want to tell others. Please help me be consistent in praying for this list, as I seek to share it with the right people at the right time. In Jesus' name, amen.

FRESH START LIST

M ake a list of people you know who need Jesus as the Hero of their life. It can be friends, family members, or even people you pass every day. Don't limit yourself. If a name comes to mind, write it down. Over the next few days, pray for each of them. God will lead you to the first ten who will hear your Jesus story, and you can share with all of them over time.

_____

_____

_____

_____

_____

_____

_____

_____

_____

_____

Clear Perspective

Prayer shapes your thinking. Changes your perspective. Keeps you focused. This is especially important when you begin to doubt your role in God's story and ask questions like, "Will people listen?" Or, "Will I say the right words?" Even, "Will anyone actually care?"

📖 Word

> Rejoice in the Lord always. I will say it again: Rejoice! … Do not be anxious about anything, but in every situation, by prayer and petition, with thanksgiving, present your requests to God. And the peace of God, which transcends all understanding, will guard your hearts and your minds in Christ Jesus. (Philippians 4:4, 6–7)

👥 Reflect

God already knows the concerns you have about sharing your story. But if you take time to pray and turn your worry into words, he will give you peace of mind. You will see the bigger picture. His perspective will calm your fears.

➡ SHARE THIS

No matter what comes against you, pray and let God change your perspective. #tell21

🔓 Prayer

Lord, I know you'll never fail me when I put my trust in you. I really need your perspective to see beyond myself. Please give me confidence that you'll bless my obedience. Thank you for working in me and through me to help people know I care deeply about them. In Jesus' name, amen.

*Remember to be praying for the friends
on your Fresh Start List. Pay close attention
to what you hear God saying.*

Real Power

Jesus instructs his followers, "Love your neighbor" (Matthew 22:39). There are so many ways to do that, but praying for them is the most powerful. Through prayer, God has given you a weapon to break down the barriers in their lives that keep them from hearing the story of Jesus.

📖 Word

In the same way, the Spirit helps us in our weakness. We do not know what we ought to pray for, but the Spirit himself intercedes for us through wordless groans. And he who searches our hearts knows the mind of the Spirit, because the Spirit intercedes for God's people in accordance with the will of God. And we know that in all things God works for the good of those who love him, who

have been called according to his purpose.
(Romans 8:26–28 NIV)

👥 Reflect

Sometimes you might struggle with exactly what to say when you pray. That's okay. God hears you even when you can't vocalize your thoughts. He knows your heartbeat. His Spirit communicates your feelings even if you can't speak. Don't be afraid to be silent. He's still at work even when you lack words.

➦ SHARE THIS

The power of prayer is best experienced not explained. #tell21

🔓 Prayer

Lord, there are days when I feel powerless. Times in prayer when I am speechless too. I thank you for your Spirit, who communicates to me and through me even when words don't come. I know that will be the case when I share my story as well. Thank you for always being in control. In Jesus' name, amen.

Remember to be praying for the friends on your Fresh Start List. Pay close attention to what you hear God saying.

CHECKPOINT

You've just finished the first several days of praying about this assignment. The foundation has been laid for an exciting second week. Before we tackle the next chapter of this life-saving saga, it's time for reflection. Answer the following questions:

1. What has God been teaching me about my prayer life this week?
2. What have I discovered about myself by listening to God's voice?
3. What people has God laid upon my heart more than others so far?

Talking to God for the benefit of others is called "intercessory prayer." It kind of means "bargaining on others' behalf." There's no greater expression of love than pleading someone's case before the Creator. This helps during *Tell21* and beyond.

Here are five ideas to help you become a world-class prayer machine:

+ **Make it regular:** Set time aside every day. Actually write it into your schedule.

+ **Make it a priority:** Don't let other plans become an excuse for missing the meeting.

+ **Make it about God:** Be humble and mindful of the majesty of your real audience.

+ **Make it thankful:** Gratitude is a good way to begin communication with God.

+ **Make it motionless:** Stop all other activity. Be still and give God your full attention.

These five steps are only a starting point to strengthening your prayer life. Consistency is the key. You will be amazed how much you long to seek God and how sweet it is to bring the needs of others before him. Make intercessory prayer a daily habit.

Don't stop praying. Keep referring to page 21. You're seeking God's leading for who's ready to hear the story he's preparing for you to share. Be diligent. Trust him to open their heart.

💡 Spotlight

It was Christmastime in a nation where 80 percent of the people were Muslim. The story of Jesus' birth was a foreign idea to most. So churches united to give people a book that explained the message of the Christ child who would become the world's Hero.

Twelve-year-old Reuben saw an opportunity here. This was his chance to tell friends and neighbors about his part in God's bigger picture. It was his time to be a light for Jesus—the story's main character.

Reuben knew he could help, so he requested two thousand books be delivered to him personally. But when they arrived, he wasn't able to even carry them from the bus stop. There was no one to help. His pastor was away, and his dad didn't want to be bothered. Reuben couldn't find anyone who understood the importance of his assignment in this life-saving saga and was willing to give him a hand. As a last resort, he told his mom, "Hey, I'll trade getting Christmas gifts this year, if you'll help me move the books." She agreed. It was an easy decision and a worthy sacrifice in order to share the story of God's gift to the world with people in his community.

Reuben made a plan. He used all the money from his savings account to put on each book a sticker bearing the name of his church. On Christmas day, he set out with armful after armful of them. All by himself, he shared the message of Jesus with two thousand homes and families.

God blesses sacrifice. He loves it when we put people first. That's what this tale is all about anyway—loving others enough to care, no matter the cost. Learn from Reuben. Let your light shine and illuminate the real star of the story—Jesus.

📖 Word

In the same way, let your light shine before others, so that they may see your good works and give glory to your Father who is in heaven. (Matthew 5:16)

SHARE THIS

Prayer unlocks the hardest hearts. #tell21

Journal

Journal

Journal

Week 2

CARE

Care

It's time to build on the groundwork you laid during the first week. The focus shifts from prayer to care. Both are practical. Necessary. And require real faith.

When you communicate with God through prayer, you believe he's listening. Even though you can't physically see or touch him, you're confident he's paying attention. And you hope he will respond in a relevant way.

In the same way, people's lives communicate needs as well. Their actions and words express deficiencies and desperation. Just like you hope God will intervene for the issues you bring to him in prayer, people want you to see and hear their hurts and notice their deepest needs. Caring is living, breathing empathy. Love in action. It's the next step in how we join God in his story. It must be hands-on and deliberate.

💡 Insight

In the first revelation God gave his human creation, found in the first book of the Bible (it's later referred to in the New Testament by Jesus as well), God said, "It is not good that the man should be alone" (Genesis 2:18). This insight goes beyond the relationship between husband and wife. It's not only about marriage but also about our responsibility to come alongside each other. It's a solution for our most basic human needs—to nurture and to provide.

Here are some common challenges people face: domestic abuse, bullying, pregnancy out of wedlock, drug use, homelessness, sexual abuse, loneliness, low self-esteem, depression, suicidal thoughts, problems in school, unhealthy relationships, pornography, alcoholism, smoking, pressure to have sex, self-harm, unemployment, financial worry, not feeling accepted, and poverty.

While this list is incomplete, it should help you see the issues that people on your list may be dealing with.

🔦 Spotlight

Jesus had a half brother named James (talk about big shoes to fill). In a letter James wrote to other Christians, he tackled this topic. He used the words *faith* and *deeds*, but it's the same idea. Care. Love in action. It's a strong challenge that will help you understand the importance of this week's emphasis.

📖 Word

What good is it, dear brothers and sisters, if you say you have faith but don't show it by your actions? Can that kind of faith save anyone? Suppose you see a brother or sister who has no food or clothing, and you say, "Good-bye and have a good day; stay warm and eat well"—but then you don't give that person any food or clothing. What good does that do? So you see, faith by itself isn't enough. Unless it produces good deeds, it is dead and useless. Now someone may argue, "Some people have faith; others have good deeds." But I say, "How can you show me your faith if you don't have good deeds? I will show you my faith by my good deeds." (James 2:14–18 NLT)

Prayer and care. That's the winning combination you need to practice if you want people to know Jesus is real and God's story applies to them. He has a part written with their name on it too. Bottom line: Set an example with your life. Let others see Jesus alive in you every day as you care for them. Give them a reason to ask you about your Hero.

Prayer and care working in tandem to prime the pump for you to share your Jesus story so others can experience freedom found only in Christ.

SHARE THIS
Care is living, breathing empathy. #tell21

As you've been praying about your list of companions who need a fresh start in Jesus, God has been prompting you. He's been putting some people on your mind more than others. Revise your list from page 23 to the ten names you feel need attention right now. Next to their name, write down a specific need they face. As you pray for them, ask God to show you how to care for each person in a relevant way.

Name & need:

_____

_____

Name & need:

_____

_____

Name & need:

_____

_____

Name & need:

_____

_____

Name & need:

_____

_____

Name & need:

_____

_____

Name & need:

_____

_____

Name & need:

_____

_____

Name & need:

_____

_____

Set the Example

How do you learn? Simple. You watch. Then you repeat what you see. Over time, you practice to improve. Your habit of loving others becomes a lifestyle of contagious care. People will view your actions and follow your example. So start an empathy epidemic. Be infectious. Let your life set the pace.

📖 Word

When he had finished washing their feet, [Jesus] put on his clothes and returned to his place. "Do you understand what I have done for you?" he asked them. "You call me 'Teacher' and 'Lord,' and rightly so, for that is what I am. Now that I, your Lord and Teacher, have washed your feet, you also should wash one another's feet. I have set you an example that you should do as I have

done for you. Very truly I tell you, no servant
is greater than his master, nor is a messenger
greater than the one who sent him. Now that
you know these things, you will be blessed if
you do them." (John 13:12–17 NIV)

👥 Reflect

God isn't asking you to do anything that Jesus didn't
first model. And he's not sending you without preparing you. His power is promised to you. It's your
source of strength to care for others. In Christ, you
have everything you need. You've got this!

🔗 SHARE THIS

Care deeply. Start an empathy epidemic
today. #tell21

🔒 Prayer

Lord, thank you for calling me into the cast of
your story. Thank you for the example Jesus set
through his life. Open my eyes to see the needs
of others who must know your Son. Please give
me your strength and compassion this week to
put your love to work. In Jesus' name, amen.

⊕ Care

Take some time to review your list of names and
their needs. Talk to God about each person. Write
down a couple of ways you can express genuine
care for them this week. Make a plan for how you're
going to care for the first two people on your list.

Talk Is Cheap

How often do you hear people say one thing and do another? Their mouths are moving. But that's about all. Instead, your life should be marked with words like *authentic*, *genuine*, and *true*. These are the qualities people admire. Commit to being one whose words and life align.

Word

Little children, let us not love in word or talk but in deed and in truth. By this we shall know that we are of the truth and reassure our heart before him. (1 John 3:18–19)

Reflect

When people's actions and words contradict each other, people typically label them a hypocrite. Sadly, hypocrites don't make good heroes. Jesus put words to work. You can too. Your life is a mirror that reflects your lifestyle, so make sure your walk and talk match.

SHARE THIS

Don't just talk about it. Be about it. Actions speak louder than words ever will. #tell21

Prayer

Lord, thank you for Jesus. He was the living, breathing, walking Word of God. I want that to be true of my life as I live out your story too. May my words and actions match and bring glory to you every day. In Jesus' name, amen.

Take some time to prayerfully choose the next two friends you're going to care for today. Say out loud what you're going to do. Talk ... then take action. Give your words life. Before the day is over, make time to act out your faith.

Dress for Success

Apparel companies spend serious amounts of money to get you to wear their clothing. They try to convince you that putting certain brands on your body equals success or identity. Don't fall for the lie. Learn to see people for who they really are. Don't look them up and down. The only label you need to see is this: "Child of the Most High God."

📖 Word

Put on then, as God's chosen ones, holy and beloved, compassionate hearts, kindness, humility, meekness, and patience, bearing with one another and, if one has a complaint against another, forgiving each other; as the Lord has forgiven you, so you also must forgive. And above all these put on love, which binds everything together in perfect harmony. (Colossians 3:12–14)

👥 Reflect

It's so easy to judge people based on what's on the outside. But that's not their real identity. It's the mask they wear to hide what they don't want you to see. Look at what's on the inside. See their potential. Look deeper to love deeply.

📣 SHARE THIS

I am who God says I am. Nothing can take that away. #tell21

🔓 Prayer

Lord, thank you for seeing me through the blood and righteousness of Jesus. Help me view others for who they really are. Forgive me for the times I've let the labels of the world cloud my vision and keep me from loving others. In Jesus' name, amen.

⊕ Care

Take some time to pray over your entire list of people and their needs. Schedule your good deeds for the next two people today. Put compassion, kindness, and humility to work in relevant ways as you love from the inside out.

Choose Third

Do you ever feel as if nobody notices the good things you do? That other people get attention for poor choices, but your genuine actions are overlooked? Sometimes you need to remind yourself of your real motivation. Love comes from deep within and gives you better perspective to play your part in God's story.

📖 Word

Don't just pretend to love others. Really love them. Hate what is wrong. Hold tightly to what is good. Love each other with genuine affection, and take delight in honoring each other. Never be lazy, but work hard and serve the Lord enthusiastically. ... Bless those who persecute you. Don't curse them; pray that God will bless them. Be happy with those who are happy, and weep with those who weep. Live in harmony with each other. Don't be too proud to enjoy the company of ordinary people. And don't think you know it all! (Romans 12:9–10, 14–16 NLT)

👥 Reflect

You don't need a pat on the back for caring for others. That's nothing more than cheap applause. God has a real reward in store for you that is far greater than any attaboy or attagirl anyone else could ever give you. Others may not see your deeds, but he does—always.

➡️ SHARE THIS

God gets first place. Others come second. I choose third. #tell21

🔒 Prayer

Lord, I admit it feels good to be appreciated by others. But even when no one else sees, I know you do. As I care for the people on your list, please help that be good enough for me. Thank you for letting me share your love. In Jesus' name, amen.

⊕ Care

Take some time to follow up on your good deeds from the last three days. Make sure your friends are doing fine. Then pray over your list again. Ask God which two friends are next and how to serve them best.

Follow the Leader

ho's setting the example for your life? Where is your focus?

When Jesus is your Hero, he also becomes your role model. And he gives you strength to stay the course. If you fix your eyes on Jesus and his way of living, it's easier to think less of yourself and more about others.

Word

Therefore if you have any encouragement from being united with Christ, if any comfort from his love, if any common sharing in the Spirit, if any tenderness and compassion, then make my joy complete by being like-minded, having the same love, being one in spirit and of one mind. Do nothing out of selfish ambition or vain conceit. Rather, in

humility value others above yourselves, not
looking to your own interests but each of
you to the interests of the others. (Philippians 2:1–4 NIV)

👬 Reflect

You don't have to compete and fight to get ahead
in God's story. First place is already taken by Jesus
anyway. He's the real Hero. The only competition
left is to try to outlove others today. Now that's a
task worth your best effort.

📲 SHARE THIS

To be a real leader, you must first choose
to follow Jesus. #tell21

🔓 Prayer

Lord, it's so easy to lose sight of you some
days. I forget that real leadership means helping others win. That's the person I want to be.
Thank you for understanding how hard that can
be and for giving me your strength. In Jesus'
name, amen.

✚ Care

Take some time to pray over your list. Thank God for the chance to join him in his work and show people love and care. You're down to the last two names now. Finish strong and hold nothing back. You're setting an example by following Christ.

CHECKPOINT

You've started a new way of life this week. Prayer and care have become your partners in this life-saving plot. They've been included in God's design since the story began. Take time to review the lessons you've discovered in the last few days. Ask yourself:

1. What has God been teaching me about putting love into action this week?

2. What have I discovered about myself by putting other's needs ahead of my own?

3. What can I do next to make care a daily habit in my life as I move forward?

On one of the journal pages, write down practical ideas for following up with people. Then get out your calendar and begin scheduling your next steps. Set daily reminders to care.

♀ Insight

Learning to care is a lifelong skill. There's always someone who needs to be noticed or requires a little extra attention when life gets rocky. Always keep your eyes open. Here are five ways that you can become someone people can rely upon:

1. **Be a good listener:** It's important that you understand people's problems and concerns. Actively listening to them is a great way to start.

2. **Be mindful:** Compassion starts by paying attention. Look for clues like facial expressions, energy levels, and body posture. These are good indicators.

3. **Be understanding:** Mirroring expressions is an easy way to let people know you feel their pain. Start by maintaining eye contact. Listen without interrupting.

4. **Be helpful:** Offer practical help to solve people's problems. Find resources and information on their issue and offer to give them a helping hand with a task.

5. **Be warm:** Send a little gift, write a kind note, or make a playlist of your friend's favorite

tunes. Offer a hug or slap on the back if appropriate.

📖 Word

Blessed are the merciful, for they shall receive mercy. (Matthew 5:7)

💡 Spotlight

At just fourteen years old, Elèna and her younger brother were displaced from their parents. They lived with their grandparents, although they were never really accepted in their home. So Elèna became the primary caretaker. To say the least, life was extremely difficult.

Between the pressure and pain from "home" and the bullying by kids at school, Elèna began to wonder if she really mattered. *Does anyone care about me?*

After contemplating that hard and hurtful question, she came to a false conclusion: she was alone. No one would miss her if she were gone. After all, she had been abandoned by parents and rejected by her grandparents. And her "friends" were just plain cruel to her.

This harsh reality made it easy for Elèna to make

a hard choice: she would end her life. Nobody would even notice, and she would finally feel no more pain. Sadly, suicide seemed like a solution. She would kill herself at the end of the school day. It was all worked out … until someone noticed her. Interrupted her life. And her plan.

On the very day Elèna planned to take her life, someone gave her a book. Then he walked her through it. Answered her questions. Explained that God loved her so much that he sent his Son—for her! For the first time in her life, she felt as if someone cared. As if she had value. That she had *hope*.

Because someone cared enough to share God's story with Elèna, she found her place within it. Jesus is now her Hero. She's even connected to a local church—playing her part in the cause of Christ—all because someone decided to share.

📖 Word

All things were made through him, and without him was not any thing made that was made. In him was life, and the life was the light of men. The light shines in the darkness, and the darkness has not overcome it. (John 1:3–5)

SHARE THIS

Care enough to remove people's alone-
ness. #tell21

Journal

Journal

Week 3

SHARE

Share

You've built a bedrock of prayer and fertilized it with care. This week, you'll take another huge step and learn your own story. You need to understand what Jesus has done for you before you can explain what he can do for others. Your faith is not complete unless you share it.

Look at your faith as a story God is writing. When you made the decision to follow Jesus, it was an act of surrender. This act of surrender is an example of your trust or faith in him as your Hero. That moment was the beginning of your relationship. Telling your tale to others reveals that relationship and gives them hope as well.

♥ Insight

Sharing your story can be nerve-wracking and uncomfortable. You may not know what to say or may think no one wants to hear about Jesus. But telling your story might be as simple as the task Jesus gave the man delivered from evil spirits.

As Jesus was getting into the boat, the man who had been demon possessed begged to go with him. But Jesus said, "No, go home to your family, and tell them everything the Lord has done for you and how merciful he has been." So the man started off to visit the Ten Towns of that region and began to proclaim the great things Jesus had done for him; and everyone was amazed at what he told them (Mark 5:18–20 NLT).

It doesn't appear from the account that this guy had a polished speech in his pocket. His story doesn't even seem to be practiced. Obviously, his monologue wasn't perfect. He just told people what Jesus did for him. Pretty simple!

You might not know the exact words to say either, but don't worry. Jesus just wants you to open your mouth and express what he's done in your life. He'll take your words and use them. That's what happened to this man. Go ahead and look at the end of his story again: "and everyone was amazed at what he told them."

This is the final piece of *Tell21*. It's the final element to help you prepare for your performance in God's story. In the next few days, you'll look at different ways you can share the story of Jesus and offer freedom-filled hope to others.

Everyone's different, so during this week, trust that God will give you insight and understanding to see the story he's writing in your life. Believe you can be a light Jesus will use to bring others into his story of redemption.

And don't stop praying and caring while learning ways to share.

 SHARE THIS

Your faith is not complete unless you share it. #tell21

Origins

*E*veryone's story has a beginning, even if they chose to follow Jesus at a young age. It's the moment their life changed when they were able to understand what Christ did for them.

Many people grow up living *as* a Christian, but they don't actually know Christ personally. A wise man once said, "God has no grandchildren." Why's that? Because it's impossible to be in a personal relationship with Jesus solely because your parents know him. Jesus said, "You must be born again" (John 3:7).

📖 Word

This week's Bible text is John 4:1–45. Take time to read the passage now using your Bible, or you can find it online. Follow the encounter of the Samaritan woman meeting Jesus face-to-face.

👥 Reflect

God is always present in our lives and working to reveal himself, even when we try to hide. Can you see the exact moment when the Samaritan woman realizes who Jesus is? How do you think her life changed after she met him? Can you identify with her story in any way?

🔗 SHARE THIS

If people can't see God around them, maybe it's because we aren't being intentional about reflecting his love. #tell21

🔒 Prayer

Lord, I praise you for the people you've placed in my life when I was spiritually thirsty. May I never forget how they showed me your love. I'm so grateful to know Jesus as the Living Water of my life. Help me be quick to see when others are thirsty and in need of you. In Jesus' name, amen.

⊕ Care

Take time today to notice the people around you who seem to need a kind word. Make their day with a simple compliment or word of encouragement.

Share

What was your life like before you ran into Jesus?
How did you first encounter him? What has your
life been like since? Think about your origin story.
How could you share it with someone today?

Day 17

Trials

Have you been or are you going through a rough time? Many people read about the Samaritan woman at the well and reduce her reputation to that of a prostitute. Jesus saw so much more in her. He saw her pain. He saw her pursuit to find purpose and meaning. Because of her reputation, she was hiding at the well during the hottest part of the day. She knew no one would be there, but Jesus was there. Ready to rescue her.

📖 Word

He told her, "Go, call your husband and come back." "I have no husband," she replied. Jesus said to her, "You are right when you say you have no husband. The fact is, you have had five husbands, and the man you now have is

not your husband. What you have just said is
quite true." (John 4:16–18 NIV)

👥 Reflect

God sees our pain and always has a purpose for our
trials. Even if they don't have a storybook ending,
they always point to God's faithfulness to never
leave us in the midst of our suffering. He's present in every storm or struggle. We're never really
alone.

🔗 SHARE THIS

You can't hide from God, so don't play hard
to get. #tell21

🔓 Prayer

Lord, I can be pretty good at hiding my pain
from others, but I know you always see my
hurts. Help me to see you even in my darkest
days. Teach me to believe that you're always in
control. I never need to hide from you. In Jesus'
name, amen.

⊕ Care

As you wander through your day, watch for people who appear to be hurting or may be even hiding their pain. Go out of your way to meet them in their loneliness. Show an interest in their life.

👥 Share

Think about your personal trial story. Consider how God never left you as you went through it. Telling the story of God's presence in the midst of your storm gives others hope. It might be the nudge they need to trust him.

Revelations

evelation is a powerful moment when God shows himself and his thoughts to us in a new way. You can easily look back on these times as turning points in your life. If you trace your experience backward, leading to an aha moment, you will often discover that God was preparing your heart for a deeper relationship with him. That's his goal for our lives—for us to know him more.

📖 Word

The woman said to him, "I know that Messiah is coming (he who is called Christ). When he comes, he will tell us all things." Jesus said to her, "I who speak to you am he." (John 4:25–26)

Reflect

Here's a list of emotions you might feel leading up to a revelation moment in your life: shock, surprise, confusion, shame, or curiosity—just to name a few. Sound familiar at all? Quite often, God reveals himself when we least expect it.

SHARE THIS

God will make a way when there seems to be no way. #tell21

Prayer

Lord, I know my feelings aren't right or wrong; they just are. But I don't want to miss what you're saying during emotional times. Teach me to hear your voice as you prepare my heart for deeper spiritual growth. In Jesus' name, amen.

Care

Ask two people questions about themselves today. Try to discover something you never knew. Don't talk about yourself. Just listen. You'll make their day!

👥 Share

Think about your revelation story. Can you see a
moment in your life when you experienced some
of the emotions above that led to a much greater
understanding of Jesus' love for you? How did this
revelation change your life? Your revelation story
needs to be shared with someone. Who could it be?

Service

When serving Jesus, you find yourself going places you wouldn't usually go and doing things you wouldn't typically do. The Samaritan woman left the scene so quickly that she forgot her water jar. She went to tell the people in the city about Jesus. It must've freaked her neighbors out to see this previously private woman acting so boldly in public.

📖 Word

Just then his disciples came back. They were shocked to find him talking to a woman, but none of them had the nerve to ask, "What do you want with her?" or "Why are you talking to her?" The woman left her water jar beside the well and ran back to the village, telling everyone, "Come and see a man who told

me everything I ever did! Could he pos-
sibly be the Messiah?" So the people came
streaming from the village to see him. (John
4:27–30 NLT)

Reflect

God has written you into his story to be his "hands
and feet" and make Jesus known in the world. Our
personal stories of service don't just reveal our abil-
ities; they also show how God is working through
his people to rescue and restore a hurting world.

SHARE THIS

Jesus died for you in public, so don't only
live for him in private. #tell21

Prayer

Lord, I need to get out my comfort zone. That's
the example you gave when you sent your Son
into our world. Help me to follow in his footsteps.
Please lead me into new situations to serve you
by serving the needs of others. In Jesus' name,
amen.

⊕ Care

Be intentional in looking for loneliness in others today. Go out of your way to find it, if necessary. You could start a conversation with a stranger or make a new friend.

👥 Share

Has God worked through you to help someone in need? Have you seen others come to Christ simply because your service to them opened their heart? Look for ways to enter someone's world. It will open doors.

Day 20

Reconciliation

Reconciliation is simply the process of rejoining things that had previously been separated. It's taking something broken and putting it back together. Restoring it. And Jesus is the master of restoration. You see it when the Samaritan woman's life is put back together. Her story connects her city to Jesus. And they're put back together too.

📖 Word

Many Samaritans from the village believed in Jesus because the woman had said, "He told me everything I ever did!" When they came out to see him, they begged him to stay in their village. So he stayed for two days, long enough for many more to hear his message and believe. Then they said to the woman, "Now we believe, not just because of what

80

you told us, but because we have heard him ourselves. Now we know that he is indeed the Savior of the world." (John 4:39–42 NLT)

👥 Reflect

Jesus died to restore the world to God. When you accepted him as your Hero, you entered the story 100 percent reconciled to the Author. It's a permanent bond that repairs your relationship with God and removes your sin from his sight.

> ### ↗ SHARE THIS
> God sees beyond who you are, to who you can become. #tell21

🔓 Prayer

Lord, I come to you in prayer because Jesus made it possible on the cross. He remodeled my life and restored my relationship with you. Let me show others the freedom they can have by being reconciled to you through him. In Jesus' name, amen.

⊕ Care

Do you have a relationship that's fading or has failed due to your words or actions? Have you hurt someone's feelings? Make it right. Start by apologizing.

👫 Share

What has happened that caused reconciliation in your life? How did Jesus restore you? Did he bring healing to a relationship? That's a powerful story. If you keep it to yourself, how will it help others?

CHECKPOINT

This week, you have read five simple ways of telling the story of Jesus in your life. Perhaps you resonate with one more than another. If you search your heart, you will find that your story can be found in each of them. Reflect on these questions:

1. What has God been teaching me about how my story fits into his story?

2. What have I discovered about my story that I didn't realize or maybe forgot?

3. What part of my story is the most powerful for telling how Jesus transformed my life?

Being able to tell your story to others starts with understanding it yourself. Go beyond these questions. Write out your story. Make sure to read it often.

♀ Insight

Telling the story of Jesus as your Hero is called a testimony. Being able to share it effectively is not difficult, but there are some strategies that can make it better. Here are a few ideas to help you tell your story so people want to listen:

* **Be brief:** Try to stick to the main points of how Jesus entered your life.

* **Be specific:** Give tangible examples. Talk about your feelings and events.

* **Be current:** Share how Jesus is working in your life today. Make it relevant.

* **Be honest:** You should never exaggerate for effect. The simple truth is best.

* **Be understandable:** Avoid using religious words that only make sense to Christians.

Remember to keep your testimony all about Jesus. Not about you. It's a before-and-after story of what he did on the cross and what he has done in your life.

📇 Word

For I resolved to know nothing while I was with you except Jesus Christ and him crucified. (1 Corinthians 2:2)

SHARE THIS

This is my story. And I will be a light. #tell21

Journal

Journal

Journal

YOUR NEXT STEPS

You lack for nothing. The Author has called you into his story and given you every tool you need to succeed when you tell others what Jesus has done in your life (2 Peter 1:3). But time is of the essence; the clock is ticking. Here's what the Bible says:

> And this is the judgment: the light has come into the world, and people loved the darkness rather than the light because their works were evil. (John 3:19)

Sad but true. And completely unnecessary. Nobody ever needs to live without the freedom and hope God offers through Jesus, who describes himself like this: "I am the light of the world. If you follow me, you won't have to walk in darkness, because you will have the light that leads to life" (John 8:12 NLT).

When you accepted Christ, he took up residence in your heart (Ephesians 3:17). He brought you from death to life and darkness to light (Romans 5:10). He's alive in you—making you fully alive.

Prayer. Care. Share. 1, 2, 3. Lather. Rinse. Repeat. The process you've practiced over the last twenty-one days is a flawless recipe. Does it mean that people will accept Jesus as their Hero the moment you share your story? Or ever? Unfortunately, no. But it does mean they will have the choice. A real chance to find their place in God's story.

Remember, the story was never about you. Your role and responsibility isn't to get others to say yes to God's invitation. That's God's job. Your assignment is simply to extend it. Yes, it will be heartbreaking if people pass on the opportunity, but don't get deterred. When you share Jesus, you plant a seed of hope in their heart. That's your part. And it's where you must trust God to take over (1 Corinthians 3:6). He's at the very center of the process. It's his story. He's the one who makes things grow.

There have been many people written into God's story who others have written off. You might even know someone considered to be a "lost cause." But here's the great news: God specializes in the impossible (Matthew 19:26). So tell your story to everyone who will listen. Stick to the plan: prayer, care, share. Don't get discouraged in doing good. At the right time, you'll see your Hero become their Hero, if you trust God and don't quit (Galatians 6:9)!

AND BEYOND

You've just finished some intense training that many people put off or ignore. But not you. There was no way you were going to run from your role in God's story. You can feel really good about your hard work. So take a deep breath. Or even take a slight bow. Just don't take a break. At least not for long, because the real fun starts now.

So what's next, exactly? Well, since you've learned your lines and better understand your part in God's plot now, it's time to act it out. This is the moment of truth when you get to step onto the stage and share your story with the world.

Maybe you just got a lump in your throat or a pit in your stomach. All of the sudden reality has set in with this realization: *I really have to do this now, don't I? I have to actually tell others about Jesus.* Before you panic and talk yourself out of God's task for you in this tale, let's do a little review for some reassurance.

Haven't you been prepping for three weeks? Haven't you been practicing for twenty-one days? The answer is yes and yes. You've been taking small steps and learning to follow the prayer, care, and share recipe. Did it kill you? Do you still have friends?

If you pause right now to reflect on everything you've learned, you have to admit that telling the story about what Jesus has done in your life won't be so difficult after all. The first time might be tough, but you'll discover that it gets easier and easier. In no time at all, it will be second nature to you. It will actually be next to impossible for you to *not* tell others about your Hero, Jesus, before long.

But there's one more thing you need to do, and it's very important. Your personal story is powerful because it's the real-life record of what Jesus has done in your world. God will use it to impact others for sure. But there's another record that reveals everything that Jesus has done for the whole world. It's the story of his life, death, burial, and resurrection, called the gospel.

There's a simple resource called *The Book of Hope*. This little booklet takes the gospel of Jesus Christ and breaks it down so anyone can understand it for their own life. (You can order copies of *The Book of Hope* from EndeavorResources.org to have on hand.) Then you'll always be ready to share your story and Jesus' when the time is right.

And timing is everything! As you listen to God and look for ways to meet people's needs, you'll know when people's hearts are ready to hear about Jesus. God's Spirit will tell you when to speak and what to say. Just never stop telling people about your Hero and the Savior of the world named Jesus. You'll help them find their place in God's life-saving saga too.

Now, go let your light shine!

🔓 Prayer

God, you love me and have a plan for my life in your story. I understand that now. So it's time for me to play my part. I want to start by making Jesus my Hero. I believe he died for me. His sacrifice on the cross frees me from my sin and gives me forgiveness. I want to use my new life to be a hero to others and share your story. Thank you for helping me now. In Jesus' name, amen.

About the Author

Timothy Eldred has been in youth ministry for over twenty-five years. His role as lead pastor of New Beginnings is just a disguise; he's a youth worker at heart. Since 2005, he's also served as president of Endeavor Ministries, which has trained millions of young leaders globally since 1881. Each year, Tim travels extensively, speaking and consulting on the biblical model of youth in ministry. His *Grow21* discipleship series books have been used by five hundred thousand teens worldwide.

Above all else, Tim's most important role takes place in Edmore, Michigan, where he and his wife of twenty-six years, Cindy, have raised their two sons to follow Jesus Christ.

Find Tim online at TimothyEldred.com
on Facebook at Facebook.com/timothyeldred
or on Twitter @timothyeldred

What am I supposed to do next? How does this Jesus thing work?

What questions do you have about your decision to follow Jesus? There should be a simple plan that explains the essentials of Christianity for young believers—a step-by-step resource with instructions to help you start right, stay strong, and finish well.

Begin21 provides directions to start your relationship with Jesus, live out your new identity in Christ, and find your voice in God's story. This book will help you develop healthy habits to create a lifestyle that lasts a lifetime. Also included are questions for reflection, challenges for action, and thoughts to explore with a mentor or trusted friend.

In just 21 days, you will find clarity and confidence as you begin to experience Christ working in you and through you to release your potential for God's purpose.

• • •

Did you know you're God's answer to someone's question? You have been created for significance and service—called to mission and ministry. Getting by is not an option. Getting by is getting lost.

This three-week experience will bring you and a spiritual mentor of your choice into a 21-day prayer partnership that will change your life. You'll read about people in the Bible who are just like you. Asking questions. Avoiding questions. People in discovery. Getting beyond just getting by. When you wrestle with their stories, you'll open doors for your journey of discovery.

You will walk away understanding that God really believes in you, and you matter to his plan. You will learn what it means to belong, so you no longer have to fake it or try to fit into this world. And you will gain confidence to experiment with your faith, risk failure, and become who God designed you to be.